20,

ERASURE POEMS OF JULES VERNE'S 20,000 LEAGUES UNDER THE SEA

JENNIFER ROCHE

QUADTYCHS BY HOSHO MCCREESH

Alternating Current Press
Boulder, Colorado

20,
Jennifer Roche
©2020 Alternating Current Press

Alternating Current
Boulder, Colorado
alternatingcurrentarts.com

ISBN: 978-1-946580-14-6
First Edition: March 2020

THE LEAGUES

*for my parents
who loved me and brought me to the sea*

THIS unexpected   stunned me   that   recollection of my sensations at the time. I was drawn down to a depth of about   feet.   swimmer (though with a   trying to rival Byron or Edgar Poe, who were   in the water, in that plunge I did not lose my presence of mind. Two vigorous   strokes   to the surface of the water.   to look for the frigate. Had the crew   the   the Abraham Lincoln veered round   and the captain put out a boat. Might I hope to be saved?

The darkness was intense. I caught a glimpse of a black mass disappearing in the east, its beacon lights dying out in the distance. It was the frigate! I was lost.

"Help, Help!" I shouted, swimming towards the Abraham Lincoln in desperation.

My clothes encumbered me; they seemed glued to my body and paralyzed my movements.

I was sinking! I was suffocating!

"Help!"

This was my last cry. My mouth filled with water. I struggled against being drawn down the abyss. Suddenly my clothes were seized by a strong hand, and I felt myself drawn up to the surface of the sea, and I heard, yes, I heard these words pronounced in my ear—

"If master would be so good as to lean on my shoulder, master would swim with much greater ease."

I seized with one hand my faithful Conseil's arm.

"Is it you?" said I, "you?"

ERASURE poetry is a conversation with an existing text as well as a new event for that text. The poet excavates words from the source to create a new poem. If done with care, the new works —the found poems—stand on their own merit and speak from their own time period, apart from the original work; the poet will have released something new.

—*Jennifer Roche*

20,

THE STRAITS

the tides lighten
and render me
an   immovable

                                        anchor

                a

                        piece of iron
sold for its weight.

                I do not despair

                flight might be possible

                , it is another thing;

                                there are trees
                                        and

        permission

AN UNKNOWN

This unexpected   stunned me

      to a depth of

Edgar Poe,

        Two vigorous

           lights

    shouted,

      My mouth filled with
          abyss.

                I heard
      in my ear —

"Is it you?"

SANDY HOOK

by three times lowering and

raising the American flag,

Sandy Hook

skirted

The dark waters of the

soul

and   would not let the men   discuss whatever

doubts they may have

      —   it was an act of faith, not logic.

The Breathing Apparatus

inhaling and exhaling

connect

me to

you

The breathing

apparatus   carried   ,

a special kind of
lantern

giving off a
continuous light. Thus equipped, I   see perfectly well.

I   believe in you

WHITENESS

Half

Our prison   is
    filled with a luminous
                    whiteness

            a   phenomenon of phos-
phorescence.   I

    , unpolished,
                                , knife in hand,
stood on the defensive.
        said I;   we are still in the dark about ourselves.

THE MAN OF THE SEAS (SYRIA)

The
      two groups

          of Syria

            will one day become continents

  of
 A somewhat nervous

       specimen

,   which a breath might shatter like a soap-
bubble

     found in the American Seas,

        and

        every description
                names

         the
        pink pearls, torn from the

          curious

           and certain

  water.

ICEBERGS

;   icebergs

clad with fur

defied

their

death.

A Canoe

I saw

a single   canoe

                              floating in open
                                    promise

                    filled with midas-ears,

          ordinary shells

What is

          discovery?

          but

                              the contemplation of our

          treasure

THE INDIAN (A GREAT LOVE)

His instinct of freedom is clear to me
amidst all the darkness   I
lit a cigar.   I
understand French;

he was   one of the sailors

We were furrowing the waters

We had a great love
long and
reviving

not a moment of ennui
we

carried a long distance

some magnificent albatrosses

LOCKED UP

You must allow yourself to be locked up

in thought   and   strange

                                                    reverie

the table   all set

                                    we don't know what
might happen.

But this is the   food we get

THE   SEA (FOR JULES VERNE)

the sea supplies all my wants.

My flocks,

sown by the hand of
the Creator of all things.

I   understand
submarine forests,

the great fucus of the
North Sea;
anemones,

I taste

extraordinary stories.

I love it! The sea is everything.

Living Infinite,

reservoir of Nature

supreme tranquility. The sea does not belong
to despots.

A Venture (America)

Abraham Lincoln harpooned   with a double blow
the heart,   the pursuit   of America

        a tortuous passage, but

    The ship's crew agreed with him.
              And eyes
              opened

A Few Days on Land

I was much impressed
       with   possession
               before   we had

     prisoners

A Horn

I fancied

a   Horn,

It was madness! I began to

burn   within

into some extreme.

I inquired

if I have well understood

existence,

not   a vessel: a

place of refuge.

The Captain of Rage

The captain   of

rage   massacred the
females, and left behind   the silence of

                                    the
                            horizon

                                    "   when he can't go
any farther, he'll stop."
"I wouldn't swear to that " I answered.

                            I did not   like   the idea of
                                                beauties

                    ruined,   destroyed

                                    falling over.

        it   would
create a

mercy

                        we would be
            guided by   instinct

WHAT THE NATIVES SAW

On the reefs,
beneath a clump of mangrove trees,
the natives

found noth-
ing new,

essentially

men perish

and   open

the window   beneath

their
footropes

THE SOUTH POLE

I rushed to the

zero
horizon.
                    I asked

                         At noon

    will the sun show himself through this fog?

        the   sky
                                    replied

            a solitary island

can

                    see its limits

AT FULL STEAM (ABRAHAM LINCOLN)

Abraham Lincoln

swam   18½ miles.

It was humiliating

; the sailors abused

The speed,
                                    the clouds

 heaved
"Well?"

                 The manometer
grew warm

                                        A cry of fury broke

                                    Abraham

Lincoln

                                will escape these
bullets.

But the shot
                     hit that infernal beast.

THE DAY

the
pulleys   haul   up

                                    the
                                    day

                    I found it excellent

                            enriched by

                    A flock of terns

                caught
                in Egypt

        and   a

Nile duck

                                    covered with
                        spots.

                        It moved as if it were just

out for a stroll

I could see

                God face to face
        sheathed in lightning

            and
                        tinted with

                                    night

What I Want to Protect

I want   to protect   the
America where people enjoy a hearty laugh

and the sea is the medium for
ideas

And

earthly animals

lobsters   and crabs

reptiles and birds

unchanging   hide in its bosom

for   millennia

ABOUT THE AUTHOR

JENNIFER ROCHE is a poet, writer, and text artist who lives in Chicago, Illinois. Her poems have appeared in or are forthcoming in *Tule Review*; *Storm Cellar*; *Footnote: A Literary Journal of History* (#2); *Oyez Review*; *Rain, Party & Disaster Society*; and *Ghost Ocean*. She was named a "Writer to Watch in 2019 & Beyond" by the Chicago Literary Guild and a 2016 Charter Oak Award Semifinalist for Best Historical writing.

ABOUT THE ARTIST

HOSHO MCCREESH is currently writing and painting in the gypsum and caliche badlands of the American Southwest. His work has appeared widely in print, in audio, and on-line.

STATEMENT

In keeping with the erasure theme, each quarter of each quadtych is meant to be largely nebulous on its own, but to make sense as the reader swims deeper into the book. The deep-sea blocks are meant as stylized "redactions," leaving only partial images and a stray word here and there. And in keeping with the urgency of modernization, the partial sea blocks also contain the sense of torn or incomplete stripes on the American flag.

ACKNOWLEDGMENTS

Three of the poems from this book, "Man of the Seas (Syria)," "A Venture (America)," and "The Sea (for Jules Verne)," were first published in *Footnote: A Literary Journal of History,* #2, published by Alternating Current Press. For this work, Jennifer was chosen as a 2016 Charter Oak Award Semifinalist for Best Historical writing.

The author wishes to thank Leah Angstman and everyone at Alternating Current Press for their enthusiastic support and beautiful production of this work. Special thanks also to Hosho McCreesh for his inspired, amazing artwork. Finally, Jennifer thanks her husband, John Svolos, for his leagues-deep love during this project and always; and her children, Zachary and Natalie, for the wonders they bring to her life every day.

COLOPHON

The edition you are holding is the First Edition of this publication.

All poems are erased from Jules Verne's *20,000 Leagues under the Sea*. Versions used: Educator Classic Library edition by Classic Press, Inc. (1968) and Bantam Books, New York (1962), translated by Anthony Bonner.

The distorted title font is Stampede, created by St Rachan. The clean title font is Chuck Noon 2, created by Twicolabs Fontdation. All other text is Athelas, created by José Scaglione and Veronika Burian. The Alternating Current Press logo is Portmanteau, created by JLH Fonts. All fonts used with permission; all rights reserved.

Cover artwork created by Leah Angstman and Ejausburg. The vintage jellyfish on the title page is in the public domain, digitized by Open Clip Art—Vectors. The erasure sample comes from the aforementioned Educator Classic Library edition. All other interior artwork was created by Hosho McCreesh, ©2020, hoshomccreesh.com.

The Alternating Current lightbulb logo was created by Leah Angstman, ©2013, 2020 Alternating Current.

Jennifer Roche's photograph was taken by Mary Rafferty, ©2020. Hosho McCreesh's photograph was taken by Freddie De La Cruz, ©2020.

All of these books (and more) are available at
Alternating Current's website: press.alternatingcurrentarts.com.

ALTERNATINGCURRENTARTS.COM

Made in the USA
Columbia, SC
19 February 2020